THE REALITIES OF MANAGEMENT PROMOTION

THE REALITIES OF MANAGEMENT PROMOTION

Marian N. Ruderman
Patricia J. Ohlott

Center for Creative Leadership
Greensboro, North Carolina

The Center for Creative Leadership is an international, nonprofit educational institution founded in 1970 to foster leadership and effective management for the good of society overall. As a part of this mission, it publishes books and reports that aim to contribute to a general process of inquiry and understanding in which ideas related to leadership are raised, exchanged, and evaluated. The ideas presented in its publications are those of the author or authors.

The Center thanks you for supporting its work through the purchase of this volume. If you have comments, suggestions, or questions about any Center publication, please contact Bill Drath, Publication Director, at the address given below.

Center for Creative Leadership
Post Office Box 26300
Greensboro, North Carolina 27438-6300

CENTER FOR CREATIVE LEADERSHIP®

CCL No. 157

Library of Congress Cataloging-in-Publication Data

Ruderman, Marian N.
    The realities of management promotion / Marian N. Ruderman, Patricia J. Ohlott
      p. cm.
    Includes bibliographical references.
    ISBN 0-912879-88-2 (pbk.)
    1. Promotions—United States. I. Ohlott, Patricia J. II. Title.
HF5549.5.P7R83 1994
658.4'07126—dc20   93-43611
                                                                  CIP

Table of Contents

Acknowledgments

This report is based on a study which took several years to conduct. Although only our names are listed as authors, there were many others who contributed to the study and to the report. We are grateful to Bill Drath, Barry Gruenberg, Len Sayles, and Bob Shively, who conducted some of the interviews. Marcia Horowitz, Jane Morrow, and Alice Warren helped to analyze the data. Debbie Nelson provided superb secretarial support for the feedback of the study results and the development of this report. Several colleagues offered comments on early drafts, which helped develop our thinking. These colleagues include David DeVries, Maxine Dalton, Bill Drath, Marcia Horowitz, Ann Howard, Bob Kaplan, Cindy McCauley, Chuck Palus, Len Sayles, Bob Shively, Mel Sorcher, Walt Tornow, Ellen Van Velsor, and Martin Wilcox. Finally, we would like to acknowledge our contacts at the companies who made it possible for us to conduct the study and the many executives who shared their promotion experiences with us.

Introduction: Comparing Statements About Promotion to How Promotions Actually Occur

Promotions, particularly management promotions, play an important role in organizations. They are a way of rewarding employees and keeping them committed to the company (Markham, Harlan, & Hackett, 1987; Rosenbaum, 1984); in fact, they are one of the more significant rewards an employee can receive. They can also be developmental because managers are thereby exposed to new and challenging learning situations (McCall, Lombardo, & Morrison, 1988, p. 131). In addition, they are a highly visible means by which an organization communicates and perpetuates its values and culture in the work force (Kennedy, 1991); employees look to see who is promoted and what they are rewarded for as a means of discerning company expectations, norms, and values. Finally, and perhaps most importantly, promotions are a primary means for the organization to deploy talent and achieve strategic goals; organizations often use management promotion to reorganize and to implement new strategic initiatives.

Despite their importance—for both organizations and individuals—we know very little about how and why most promotions occur. It is a neglected topic in the literature on personnel management (Dobson, 1988; Ferris, Buckley, & Allen, 1992). Most research in the area focuses on the individual attributes important for promotion (e.g., Beyer, Stevens, & Trice, 1980) or on the outcomes of promotions (see Markham et al., 1987, for a review) such as motivation and satisfaction. With the exception of a few studies (Beehr & Juntunen, 1990; Butterfield & Powell, 1991; Lee, 1985a, 1985b; London & Stumpf, 1983; Stumpf & London, 1981a), there has been very little work done on how actual promotion decisions are made, especially at the top-management level (Rosenbaum, 1979).

We recently conducted an exploratory study of how sixty-four promotions actually occurred in three companies, and this paper presents our findings. We have decided not to use a traditional research-paper format. (A technical description of methodology and the tabular presentation of data can be found in the Appendix.) We focus here on our findings and the issues they raise.

Our discussion will be in four parts: After a brief description of the methodology of our study, we will look at the findings in terms of the following six statements: (1) Promotions are based on individual efforts and abilities; (2) people promoted must fit established jobs; (3) formal methods are used to assess candidates for promotion; (4) there are multiple candidates for each job; (5) promotions have uniform characteristics; and (6) most organizations use similar criteria for promotion. These statements do **not** represent our conclusions but instead serve as a means of organizing the data. We will identify how each is supported or refuted by the data we collected and make reference to relevant literature when appropriate.

Following this, we will offer what we think is the beginning of a framework for a better understanding of promotion. Finally, we will discuss the implications of our findings for individuals, organizations, and future research.

The reader may wonder why we chose these particular six statements to organize the data. Certainly many others could have been chosen. In the absence of a defined body of research, many interpretations of promotion have been put forward: for instance, cynical, political, structural, and rational. Statements derived from different perspectives are often contradictory. We decided to limit the statements we used to one perspective, and we chose the rational view. We picked this perspective for two reasons. First, it is a reasonably coherent view. Based on the selection literature, it is a product of the classic psychometric approach to assessment and selection (Cook, 1988), the fundamental assumption of which is that people possess attributes that can be measured objectively and that these attributes predict work performance. Second, for a subject that has been little researched, it is one of the better known approaches to selection and promotion. Third, this perspective, which suggests that promotions are based on merit, is a familiar one to most people.

It is our hope that, in contributing to a research-based understanding of promotion, this paper will (1) help organizations employ promotion more effectively, (2) allow individual managers to assess it more realistically and thereby improve their career planning and development efforts, and (3) permit researchers to study it more easily. We also hope that the framework we offer here will be expanded and revised as further research is done.

Methodology

The goal of our study was to develop an understanding of how management promotions are actually made. The lack of research in this area may be because information on the subject is extremely sensitive, especially given the current emphasis on fairness and discrimination. In addition, companies often do not have a systematic procedure for making promotion decisions or many times do not keep good records of the process (see Butterfield & Powell,

1991). In view of these circumstances, we sought to study promotions (which we defined as a change in job level along with a commensurate increase in responsibility, accountability, and level of pay) from multiple perspectives. For each promotion, we interviewed the person promoted, the promoting boss, and the promoting boss's boss. In the majority of cases we also talked with a knowledgeable human resource representative. In addition to the interviews, we were also given access to performance appraisals and succession-planning documents relevant to the promotions. From the differing perspectives we developed a picture of the events and issues leading up to each promotion; we attempted to get as complete an understanding of it as possible. Once we developed a composite picture of each promotion we then looked across them to identify common themes and differences. (The Appendix provides further detail on the research methodology and data analysis.)

The sixty-four promotions we studied took place in three different Fortune 500 companies during the period 1986 to 1989. At least one of the companies, which we will call *ABC*, is known for the exceptional quality of its management practices. ABC has been listed among the best places for blacks and women to work. It has won awards for quality and places an emphasis on training and development. The second company, which we will call *MNO*, has also been listed as one of the best places for blacks to work and has implemented diversity training and internship programs. Although it has recently faced economic difficulties, the third company, which we will call *XYZ*, has a performance-management system which makes use of a carefully developed set of key leadership competencies. Further information on the companies will be provided below in our discussion of statement 6.

The interviews occurred anywhere from two months to two-and-a-half years after the promotion, with an average span of ten months. The cases studied were identified in each company with the help of senior human-resource professionals, whom we asked to identify typical promotions. Promotions that the human resource professionals felt were representative of promotion activity at their organization, we defined as *typical*. The decisions involved promotions to general-management levels, positions which reported directly to general management, and positions two levels below general management. Most of the managers promoted were white men, although sixteen were white women, one manager was a black woman, and seven were black men. Within each company the promotions occurred in different functions and businesses.

We conducted several analyses of the data. One analysis was to identify and categorize the reasons decision-makers gave for promotion. After looking through all the interviews of the hiring bosses, the bosses of the hiring bosses, and the human resource specialists, we identified thirty-six reasons why managers are promoted (see Figure 1; all figures may be found in the Appendix). An example of a reason is the following statement by a decision-maker: "This person had an outstanding track record; she was responsible for developing a strategy which significantly increased our share of the market." Each interview was coded so as to determine which reasons for the promotion were mentioned. For each reason listed in Table 1 (all tables may be found in the Appendix), we report the percentage of cases for which one or more of the decision-makers or human resource specialists involved in the case mentioned the reason.

A second analysis was to compare the different organizations in terms of these reasons and the other data we collected, with emphasis on understanding differences between companies. All the differences discussed in the text are statistically significant.

A third analysis was to identify some of the conditions in which promotions occurred. To accomplish this we coded the presence or absence of conditions thought to be informative about promotion dynamics: the formation of the job, career history of the candidate, relationship of the person promoted to the hiring boss, and other potential candidates.

A fourth analysis was to note methods and processes used to assess candidates. We looked at how bosses said they evaluated the candidates and what they used as indicators of suitability.

A fifth analysis was based on a running log of our ideas of how we thought decision-makers approached the promotion process. For each case we took notes on a series of questions about the process.

Finally, a sixth analysis was to group the promotions qualitatively according to similarities and dissimilarities of reasons and underlying circumstances.

As we mentioned above, this study was an exploratory one. Also, it primarily relied on retrospective accounts and is therefore subject to the limitations of human memory (we did try to offset this by having a number of informants for each case and by supplementing the interview with records data). Despite these limitations, we believe there is great value in this approach because it makes it possible to study real decisions rather than artificial scenarios.

Let us now consider the six statements derived from a rational view of promotion.

Statement 1:
Promotions Are Based on Individual Efforts and Abilities

According to the rational perspective, managers are promoted on the basis of their efforts and abilities. The assumption is that individual attributes predict work performance and that these attributes can be objectively measured by others. The person best suited for a particular job is the person whose attributes best fit the job. Business folklore supports this view; many managers believe that investments in the self, such as education and training, will pay off in career success. Organizations also support this view through the appraisal and reward process, which provides incentives for additional training, education, or individual accomplishments.

Our data suggest that there is a great deal of truth behind this statement. We found thirty-six reasons for promotion, which we put into five categories (preparation, attitudes, people skills, personal attributes, and context); four of these categories relate to individual achievements, characteristics, or ability. (See Table 1 for a list of the reasons and Figure 1 for definitions of the reasons.)

Contributions of the Individual: Preparation, Attitudes, People Skills, and Personal Attributes

The reasons cited for promotion most often fall into the category of preparation. Bosses and human resource specialists stressed that being well prepared for a job in terms of technical skills and experience is critical. One of the more common reasons for promotion provided by the different bosses and human resource specialists is a track record of success (mentioned in 61% of the cases; see Table 1). Other reasons that we classified as preparation include technical skills (50% of cases), having successfully introduced change (36%), the right combination of credentials (30%), and experience that adds utility to the group (30%; this last reason means that the manager brought with him or her the knowledge of a particular business or discipline that others in the work group were lacking).

Also frequently mentioned were reasons that can be categorized as attitudes towards work. For 38% of the managers, work ethic was mentioned. Work ethic was described by the decision-makers as being comprised of commitment, initiative, dedication, and eagerness. It was assessed by determining how much time managers put into their jobs and the new ideas and directions they proposed.

Reasons that can be categorized as skills dealing with people were also prominently mentioned. Basic interpersonal and communication skills were cited in 45% of cases; leadership or the demonstrated ability to build a team in 47% of the cases; and influence skills, by which we mean establishing credibility with other units—customers, partners, or industry representatives—in 39% of the cases. Another key variable was the comfort level of the boss or the boss's boss with the manager. Decision-makers who gave this as a reason meant that they were at ease with the manager and felt they could predict how he or she would behave. In other words, the candidate was a known quantity to the boss and was trusted by him or her. This was a factor in 44% of the cases.

Other reasons could be put into the category of personal attributes. The potential for growth as an executive was cited in 59% of cases and intelligence in 45% (intelligence was defined by decision-makers as the exercise of good judgment combined with good verbal skills). Personal strength or strength of character was cited in 29% of the cases (personal strength was assessed according to the risks people took, whether they challenged superiors, and the acceptance and resolution of tough decisions).

Some of the individual attributes decision-makers in our study identified are similar to those that previous research has shown to be critical for career advancement. (For a review of previous research, see Robertson & Iles, 1988.) For example, Howard and Bray (1988) found work interests, some personality and motivation variables, and cognitive, interpersonal, and administrative abilities to be important predictors of later management success. And Hough (1984) has found that records of past accomplishments can predict future performance for attorneys.

Contributions of the Context

Although our data confirm the substantial role that individual contributions make to promotions, they suggest that other factors by themselves and in combination with individual contributions also play key roles in promotion decisions. Many of the reasons cited for promotion fall into a fifth category: context. These reasons involve the circumstances of the promotion (see Table 2), including issues related to the opportunity structure, role of promotions in sending signals about corporate values, and long-term staffing considerations. They are important because they emphasize determinants of career progress that are as much or more a function of the situation than of the individual. Contextual reasons of one sort of another were a factor in 81% of the cases studied. Ability-related factors were mentioned in 100% of cases, suggesting a strong interplay of ability and circumstance.

Opportunity structure. Several of the contextual reasons had to do with the availability of certain organizational opportunities. Perhaps the most compelling of these reasons was being in the right place during a major restructuring of the organization. Certain people happened to have the necessary mix of skills and qualifications and were visible to the decision-makers at just the time when the job became available. This points to the interaction of the person and the opportunity structure. Forty-eight percent of the promotions occurred in the context of a reorganization. In 22% of the cases, bosses and human resource representatives specifically mentioned being in the right place during a reorganization. Several of the managers who had been promoted got a job because of a reorganization that resulted in an upgraded position. The shift in organizational structure was a driving force for the promotion. Some of the reorganizations involved downsizing, whereas others dealt with centralization or decentralization initiatives.

In one company, MNO, restructuring as the result of expansion also led to promotion. When programs and businesses expanded, the person who got promoted was the person already there. The person with experience in the business was positioned to get the upgraded or new job. For example, one woman got a promotion, in part, because a new use was developed for a product she was marketing. The new use expanded the scope of her responsibilities.

Other studies have found a similar connection between promotion and opportunity. In a study of promotions of the Senior Executive Service of the Civil Service, Butterfield and Powell (1991) found that already being in the department was strongly related to the likelihood of advancement. Being well-positioned at the time when a new position is created, or when an old one is upgraded, is associated with promotion.

Another way in which the managers in our study were in the right place at the right time was when the first choice candidate wasn't available. This didn't happen often (10% of cases), but when it did it was significant because someone who otherwise wouldn't have gotten the job at that time was selected. Occasionally a job became available because a more qualified candidate refused it or could not be released from a prior commitment. One highly-thought-of executive got a key job because the first choice couldn't be released from his current assignment. The executive who eventually got the job didn't know he was the second choice. Again, the literature provides support for this type of circumstance. In a study of situations in which assessment data does not predict promotion, Howard (1986) pointed out that sometimes managers find it more expedient to promote an available subordinate than to search for a more promising candidate.

Promotions as signals. Another set of reasons for promotion, which didn't focus primarily on candidate abilities, had to do with the role of promotion as a means of sending signals to the organization. Many executives recognized that their subordinates looked at whom was promoted in order to interpret organizational values or how the organization should grow strategically. Thus, they were interested in the messages promotions sent, and the message influenced the choice of candidates. For example, one general manager explained that part of the reason he promoted a particular person was because the candidate had been in the division for some time and other recent assignments had gone to outsiders. He admitted that he could have found someone better from the outside, but it was critical to him that he demonstrate to insiders that he valued them.

Sometimes the message sent had to do with the value of a particular function. One of the companies, XYZ, had interdisciplinary project-work-groups. As part of a quality initiative, the work of one function was upgraded in order to demonstrate how highly this function was valued. The people performing it in the different projects got promotions because the senior executives wanted to emphasize the importance of the function in order to improve project quality.

In several of the promotions (19%; see Table 1) the signal that was sent related to the company's responsibility to the individual: The person got the promotion in part because he or she had been freed from other assignments and was available to take on a new responsibility. For example, one manager had been sent to the Far East for an important job. While he was overseas, his company reorganized the Far East division and eliminated his position. When he was brought back to corporate headquarters the company wanted to send the message, "If you move halfway across the world for us, and it doesn't work out, we will take care of you." They found him another position. Another way people became available was through divisions being sold or roles in joint ventures being phased out. In all these cases, senior management wanted to convey that they would take care of employees if their jobs disappeared. Obviously these managers were considered valuable assets to the company, but the timing of the promotion was not a consequence of their abilities.

Long-term staffing goals. When long-term staffing goals were a consideration, promotions didn't necessarily go to the person most qualified for a job at a particular point in time. For example, organizations sometimes used assignments for developmental purposes and gave key jobs to someone who needed the opportunity to refine and develop his or her abilities. Derr, Jones, and Toomey (1988) have found that assignments are commonly used as developmental interventions. Promotions take both short-term and long-term needs into account. In 47% of cases we found that developmental considerations were important factors in the decision (see Table 1). The developmental candidate was given the job because of the potential contributions he or she could make, both in the new job and future jobs. For instance, one key decision-maker said of the person he promoted to an influential spot, "He wasn't at the top of the list in terms of experience, but we decided to go with him because he has the potential to make general manager one day, maybe even president." This candidate got a key manufacturing position without ever having been a plant manager, the typical prerequisite for the job, but the people who promoted him felt he could do the job anyway because of his exceptional intelligence and leadership skills. The hiring manager decided to go with someone who in the long run was more likely to give more back to the company even though the safe choice would have been to select an existing plant manager. In companies ABC and MNO, these developmental goals were considered especially important. Not only were jobs used to develop new skills but they also served as a means of testing the candidate for future positions.

Bosses also used promotions as a way of retaining people for the long term. In a small number of cases (14%), one of the reasons a manager got a new job was for retention. The manager may have not been the best candidate for that specific job but was generally good enough that the company wanted to keep him or her because of the high likelihood of future contributions. Sometimes the company created a promotion to accommodate an employee's personal needs, such as a request for a certain location. Other times a promotion was given to console someone for not getting a job he or she really wanted. At two of the companies, ABC and MNO, people who had lobbied for a particular job were given a promotion to another job as a means of compensating them for being passed over for the opportunity they really wanted.

We also found reasons for promotion that were associated with long-term goals for diversity. The three companies placed different emphases on diversity, and this was reflected in the reasons given for promotion. Companies ABC and MNO had strong initiatives for increasing the demographic diversity of the top-management team. In both, the CEOs had publicly stated that increasing the number of men and women of color and white women entering into the senior ranks was a key goal. Therefore demonstrating support for the diversity initiative was sometimes given as a reason for promotion—but it was always mentioned in connection with performance factors such as track record and abilities such as intelligence. No one appeared to be promoted simply because of his or her demographic status. Thus, the emphasis on diversity forced managers to consider people whom they might have otherwise overlooked. The timing of the diversity emphasis encouraged the largely white-male population of bosses to consider people whom might not ordinarily have been considered.

Two other contextual reasons related to long-term staffing came up at just one company we studied, ABC, the only one where we were able to get a comparatively large sample of white-female (14) and black-male managers (5). Specifically, at this company, lobbying for the job and a commitment to equity were cited as reasons for promotion, and they were cited more often for these managers than for the white males. In fact, these are reasons for promotion that don't typically emerge when the careers of white males are studied.

When individuals lobbied or pushed for the job, we found that they had already been working for the hiring boss before they got the promotion. At first, they were put in at a level below the customary level for that job and they were told that if they did extremely well, they would then get a promotion. To some extent, the first job was described as an apprentice or trial period; some managers had titles that included the term *assistant* or *acting*. The people in these jobs felt that they had proved themselves and they had to actively campaign to get the next promotion to a job which was simply an extension of the first. For example, one woman had been promised she would be promoted a level soon after she took her job. When no promotion seemed to be forthcoming, she repeatedly asked her boss when it would happen. He kept saying, "Soon." Finally, she sent him a memo with the Webster's dictionary definition of *soon*.

With respect to equity, which bosses sometimes cited as a reason, a promotion was essentially an attempt to rectify a past mistake. These people were certainly considered deserving, but for one reason or another they didn't get a promotion in the past. The bosses said that one of the reasons they promoted the candidate was to remedy an unfair situation. When one woman took on a job as a marketing manager she started at a lower level than her male predecessor and her company told her that eventually she would be promoted. This finally came about eighteen months later when her boss got a new boss who felt she was undervalued compared to people in similar positions. Although she was clearly an important contributor, part of the reason why she was promoted was to remedy her unfair situation. This type of promotion did not happen exclusively to white women and to women and men of color, but this is the population in which we first noticed it because it occurred with a relatively high frequency.

Prior research has addressed gender as a factor in promotion. Numerous studies have documented that different processes or criteria are used in the promotion of women and men (Beehr & Juntunen, 1990; Butterfield & Powell, 1991; Cannings, 1988; Cannings & Montmarquette, 1991; Eberts & Stone, 1985; Gold & Pringle, 1988). This sort of information, however, is rarely incorporated into the literature on promotion and personnel selection (Forbes & Piercy, 1991, is a notable exception). By looking at people traditionally excluded from upper-management roles, some of the circumstantial factors in promotion become more apparent. In one company, ABC, the timing of women's promotions appears to be different than the timing of promotions for men.

The Complete Picture: Individual and Contextual Reasons for Promotion

There are many reasons why people get promoted. Much of the research on career advancement has focused on the knowledge, skills, and abilities that managers must hold in order to get ahead (e.g., Howard, 1986; Robertson & Iles, 1988). These are features of the individual that qualify them for advancement. And individual attributes are commonly thought to be key factors in promotion.

Our research with decision-makers has supported the notion of the criticality of individual attributes, efforts, and achievements. It has also shown that the picture is incomplete. The bosses and human resource specialists we interviewed offered many situational reasons for promotion. Although bosses always viewed the managers they promoted as talented and well-prepared, it was often the context—especially the opportunity structure, desire to reinforce values, and long-term staffing considerations—that drove the promotion. Individual qualities are important but their importance is often subtly tied to features of the situation. This supports the conclusions of Rosenbaum (1989a) and Veiga (1973), who have identified the critical role opportunity plays in promotion. Getting ahead requires more than simply having the right qualities.

Statement 2:
People Promoted Must Fit Established Jobs

Another rational view is that people are promoted into established, stable jobs. Standard personnel-selection advice is that jobs should be analyzed in terms of the knowledge, skills, and abilities required to do them (Schneider & Schmitt, 1986), with these requirements forming the basis for selection criteria. A related assumption is that the best person for the job is the one who can most effectively demonstrate the knowledge, skills, and abilities called for; in other words, the best person is the one who best fits the fixed requirements of the job. This makes sense in theory, but in practice we found that jobs at the managerial level are dynamic. Our data suggest that often a job is adapted to fit the candidate, through customizing established jobs, creating new jobs, or promoting people who are expected to enact a job in a certain way.

We found in 20% of the cases that the job had been somehow customized to meet the needs or capitalize on unique strengths of the individual (see Table 2). One candidate, for example, had been considered one of the higher-potential people in a corporate staff function. To broaden him, he was given an assignment that required his playing more of a line-management role. This assignment, however, did not work out. In order to save him for the corporation they created a new job that capitalized on his special area of expertise, a particular business-analysis skill. In another case, a customized job was provided for someone likely one day to head up an administrative function. This special job was an "assistant function head" position that would give the manager, a mid-career hire, necessary experience. When he leaves the position, it is likely to remain unfilled unless someone else has a developmental need for this type of position.

Another kind of job customizing that we noted was when a manager had expanded an existing job and the promotion was an acknowledgment of the situation. Yet another occasion of customization was when a prime reason for a promotion was to recognize the increased skills of the person.

Sometimes jobs were new and hiring managers couldn't fully define them. In these cases we found that hiring managers looked for people who were generally good and then let those candidates define the job themselves. How the job eventually got shaped was as much a function of the incumbent, who got considerable input into the design of the job, as it was of business needs. In one case the new job involved gaining technical information from outside the company. Much of how this was carried out was up to the incumbent. The hiring boss realized that the job would be enacted differently depending on the person who moved into it.

Another way that we found that jobs were adaptable related to the way old and new responsibilities were combined. At ABC there is a tendency for people taking on a new role to take some old responsibilities with them. Thus we encountered some strange combinations of responsibilities. One person was both CFO of a tangential business and in charge of managing a major corporate administrative program. We found people with information-processing responsibilities and personnel-management duties, and people with both staff and line functions, because they were given the chance to try out a new discipline while devoting some of their time to something old and familiar. Many of the jobs existed in the configuration we saw at only one particular point in time.

In summary, the nature of the job influenced, but did not determine, selection criteria for these positions. To some extent the manager defined the job. Job skills and requirements did not always drive who was selected. Instead, the proposed incumbent's talents helped to define and shape the job.

Statement 3:
Formal Methods Are Used to Assess Candidates for Promotion

When it comes to promotion decisions, one of the basic tenets of the rational view is that it is possible to predict future organizational contributions. The assumption is that qualities of the individual can be objectively assessed and used to predict future performance. Various organizational processes and procedures have been developed to facilitate prediction of managerial contributions. These systems include assessment centers, performance appraisal, and succession-planning systems. Each of these aims to provide accurate and reliable data about job-holders. The validity of many of these practices, particularly assessment centers and psychological tests (Bentz, 1990; Bray & Howard, 1983; Howard & Bray, 1988), is quite good (see Robertson & Iles, 1988, for a review). It is reasonable, then, to assume that this data would be used as a basis for promotion. Studies of the types of information decision-makers prefer (Taylor, 1975), as well as studies of the factors considered in simulated promotions (Stumpf & London, 1981a), suggest that data from formal systems are used by decision-makers.

We found, however, that these formal ways of collecting data received mixed reviews from the executive decision-makers (bosses and their bosses). Not one of the three companies used assessment centers at this level, but all three had performance-appraisal and succession-planning systems. The executives occasionally reported that they had incorporated formally collected data into the decision—typically the information about specific accomplishments shared at succession reviews. The reviews appeared to be places where opinions about candidates were shared and solidified.

The reviews are used more at MNO than at the other two companies. Part of the reason for this is that this company has a history of its CEO and division presidents being influential in promotion decisions way down the line. When they get involved in a decision a few levels removed, they use the data collected in the people reviews to convince subordinate managers to take a chance on unfamiliar candidates. This was the case when the president or CEO tried to convince executives to take on a manager from another division. For moves across businesses, this review information was valuable. In most cases, though, formally collected data didn't enter into the promotion decision.

In part, the formal data was not used because of the difficulty of assessing middle-management work. By its very nature middle-management work is ambiguous. Ferris and King (1991) have shown that as hierarchical level increases, so does the ambiguity of the work, thus making it difficult to delineate criteria. Several of the bosses interviewed complained about the difficulty of teasing out the performance of one particular manager in situations with team efforts, large time frames, and difficult business decisions.

We did ask decision-makers what information they used when making a promotion decision. Essentially, hiring bosses relied on an intuitive, subjective process that concentrated on their personal knowledge of the candidate and opinions of others (bosses, former incumbents of the job, peers, and former supervisors of the candidates). Similar to what other studies have found (Butterfield & Powell, 1991; London & Stumpf, 1983), many of the candidates had worked in the department (69%) or had prior work relationships with the boss or the boss's boss. These prior relationships formed a critical source of information about the candidates.

Bosses described past relationships as giving them insight into three things in particular: (1) past accomplishments, (2) potential, and (3) comfort level. From the past working relationships, bosses predicted future success.

We found that—as Forbes (1987), Forbes and Piercy (1991), and Rosenbaum (1984, 1989b) suggested—decision-makers rely on earlier signals of ability in order to make decisions about future moves. Bosses gave past job accomplishments as evidence of managerial competence. Usually the past accomplishments were relatively recent and involved the introduction of change. The changes that promoted managers had made took many forms: implementing quality programs, making technical breakthroughs, improving a record-keeping system, developing a creative way to expand the customer base, improving operations, and contributing to the corporate community. These changes were highlighted as reasons for promotion.

Another quality that was strongly emphasized in the assessments of bosses is potential. This is the basic belief that the candidate would prove able to handle the next-level job. In addition, potential was often described in terms of a candidate's personal attributes—intelligence, character, and style. The candidate's intelligence was seen as a signal of future ability. Most bosses were confident in their ability to judge potential and relied on assessments of how well the person came across in presenting and defending his or her own ideas.

A common explanation for this confidence was the boss's level of comfort with a particular candidate—that is, if the boss felt that he or she worked well with and trusted the candidate. Several decision-makers explained that, given the uncertainty of the business situations and the difficulty of making predictions, they wanted someone they knew and could trust. For example, one boss said, "I came here in 1962 and he came in 1964. I was an engineer with him in the same group at that time and I know what he can do. I've known him for twenty-five years and am very compatible with him." Comfort with the candidate was mentioned in 44% of the cases (see Table 1). This means that the boss promoted the manager in part because, given the ambiguity of managerial work, the boss felt comfortable that the candidate could do the job. Promoting a known quantity was a way to minimize risk in the face of business uncertainty.

In many cases the personal knowledge about candidates was gathered over a number of years. This was particularly true at the most bureaucratic company studied, XYZ, where it was not unusual for a boss to have known the person promoted for twenty or more years. In other cases the relationship between the boss and promoted manager was less extensive and may have amounted to only an acquaintance based on attendance at meetings, presentations, or written reports. In such instances the bosses often supplemented their personal knowledge with the second major source of information, reputational information. This was referred to as "the collective mind," "the hiring brain," "the book," or "hall talk," with the name of the internal-reputational data base varying by company and division. This is the type of information that is informally passed through networks. Not all such talk is equal. Decision-makers were sensitive to who the source of the information was. The better the reputation of the reference, the better the candidate was thought of. In the words of one of the promoted managers, "If your reputation comes from someone respected in the organization, it counts for much more than if someone not respected thinks a lot of you." One promoted manager was described as having earlier in his career received a "love note" from the president and this helped his recognition over the years.

In one company, ABC, managers were relatively systematic about getting data; they sought the opinions of internal clients, peers, or former bosses of the candidates. This company also had a comparatively large staff of human resource specialists to assist executives in collecting data from former bosses and colleagues.

In summary, although the rational perspective sees objective assessment as a prerequisite for promotion, the bosses interviewed in our study suggest that middle-management work is amorphous and difficult to assess objectively. Bosses didn't place much emphasis on formally collected data, such as performance appraisals, and instead relied on an individualized assessment process based on signals of ability, past accomplishments, intelligence, and comfort level.

Statement 4:
There Are Multiple Candidates for Each Job

One of the assumptions of the rational perspective is that there are usually multiple candidates for a position. The purpose of the selection decision is to pick the best person from the applicant pool.

Our study found that often there was only one true candidate; in 43% of the cases the decision-makers considered only one person (see Table 2). One reason for this is that jobs were frequently built around a person. As discussed above, some jobs were created to capitalize on a particular individual's strength. In other cases there was an expansion of job responsibilities, so only one person was a logical candidate.

A second explanation for this phenomenon is that only one person may have had the basic qualifications. Managers at all three companies had reservations about the size of the talent pool. Thus, a real or perceived lack of prepared candidates may be why there was limited competition. Although talented people may exist in the candidate pool, hiring managers may not know them well enough to discern their promotable qualities.

A third reason is the grooming of candidates. In several cases a particular candidate was groomed over a period of several years for a particular job, so when there was an opening he or she was the designated manager to fill it.

A fourth reason is the proximity to the decision-maker. In 73% of the cases, the person promoted had either worked with the hiring manager or the hiring manager's boss or both. (Table 2 shows percentages for hiring manager and hiring manager's boss separately, but there was overlap between them.) Thus they were very visible to the decision-makers. Kanter (1977) has documented the importance of visibility to advancement in one large organization. Being known by the hiring parties at the time an opportunity becomes available may explain why there often is only one candidate. Bosses don't feel compelled to look elsewhere if they know of someone capable who is already familiar with the work and the personalities involved. In a study of simulated decision-making, London and Stumpf (1983) found that proximity to the decision-maker increased the likelihood of promotion. In 81% of our cases, the people promoted had a career-facilitating relationship with someone higher in the organization who helped their visibility.

There was, however, variation with regard to the number of candidates across companies. The percentage of cases with multiple candidates was 18% in ABC, 80% in XYZ, and 83% in MNO. (These numbers were computed after asking decision-makers about other candidates for the promoted person's job. They do not appear in the Appendix.) The difference may relate to cross-functional or cross-business moves. MNO puts a greater emphasis on such moves and consequently tends to consider more candidates per position. The largest number of candidates considered for a single position was ten. In one case when this happened there was a downsizing going on. In another, it was a premier job considered to be both influential and developmental, and the decision-makers wanted to ensure they got the best person.

In summary, although there were often multiple candidates for a job, in nearly half the cases there was only one person considered.

Statement 5:
Promotions Have Uniform Characteristics

The rational perspective, not to mention business folklore and most of the literature on staffing decisions, views promotions as if they were all alike. In interviewing for this study, we found a tremendous variety in the types of promotions. They differ in terms of how the vacancy develops, the number of candidates considered, corporate objectives for the person or position, and whether the chosen candidate has been groomed or mentored. To better understand the variation in strategies, we grouped the promotions from the three companies into five types according to their underlying features: developmental promotions, promotions in place, promotions for which there was no obvious candidate, promotions to advance long-term corporate objectives, and promotions resulting from reorganizations (see Table 3 and Figure 2). The promotions in each category had more in common with each other than with those in the other categories.

Developmental Promotions

Developmental promotions were the most common. The underlying idea here was that a promotion would help a person prepare for key positions in the future. Thirty-one percent of the promotions we studied fit this description (see Table 3). Most of these were part of a natural career progression where a candidate was earmarked for a job that he or she had been prepared for, and that was intended to prepare that person for future jobs in the business or function. They were considered high-potential candidates, and many of them had mentors.

One of the companies, MNO, made some developmental promotions that were relatively high risk. Managers were moved to positions their bosses considered to be big developmental gambles—in one case a move of two levels, in another a single-level move combined with a new function. These promotions strongly emphasized long-term over short-term needs and placed people with important credentials missing in their backgrounds into specific jobs in an effort to broaden their skills. Decision-makers, especially those higher than the hiring boss, definitely felt the risk was worth taking in these cases because the payoff to both the individual and organization could be great.

Promotions in Place

In contrast to developmental promotions, in which the managers moved to new or different jobs, were promotions in place. In such a situation there was, of course, only one true candidate. As mentioned above, sometimes the person expanded the job and got a promotion to acknowledge the increase in responsibilities; in other cases the candidate had enhanced his or her repertoire of skills and the promotion was an acknowledgment of increased abilities. Obviously, all of the managers promoted in place knew the boss and hiring boss well. In almost all of these cases the promotion required creating a new job title.

Promotions With No Obvious Optimal Candidate

Unlike promotions in place, in which there was a single candidate, there were promotions for which there was no obvious optimal candidate. Jobs existed and there was a departmental need to fill them. There were several responses to this situation. One was to search for a single stellar candidate. Another was to get multiple candidates. Some bosses did this through word of mouth; others used the formal system. XYZ had a job-posting system that encouraged candidates to apply for certain-level jobs. In one case the hiring boss was pleasantly surprised by the people who applied, and he eventually hired someone unfamiliar to him who was much better than any of the managers he personally knew or who were referred to him.

Sometimes the searches for quality candidates were unsuccessful from the boss's perspective and the boss had to hire someone he or she had misgivings about. In one situation, the hiring boss's boss said that the job was boring and that it wasn't perceived as a way to get ahead. He couldn't find any outstanding candidates for it, so he hired someone who had limited potential.

Promotions for Long-term Corporate Objectives

Many promotions related to long-range staffing goals. They usually had some involvement by the boss's boss or human resources, and their purpose was to ensure that a particular candidate received a good position. Some of the candidates were simply jobless and available through no fault of their own. As discussed above, they had been reorganized out of a job, their division had been sold, or an overseas assignment had come to an end. The company did not want to lose them, nor did it want to send the message that a manager will be "forgotten" if he or she travels to a distant location. A special effort was made by the organization to get these people placed. Many of these promotions were across business lines. In several cases the hiring boss was strongly encouraged to choose the person.

Promotions made to retain people can also be seen as connected to long-term staffing objectives. There were managers who had indicated that they wanted to leave and the company created a job to meet their needs as a way of keeping them for the future.

Another long-term staffing objective for which promotions were made was the implementation of diversity. ABC and MNO were actively trying to increase diversity in the leadership ranks. In these companies some highly qualified white women and men and women of color were promoted to help prepare them for future positions. The managers in this group were considered to be of the highest potential and their careers were monitored closely. The process was similar to that often engaged in for the highest-potential white males; however, these promotions were more visible because they provided evidence of commitment to the diversity programs.

Promotions Resulting from Reorganization

Finally, we found promotions resulting from a reorganization. XYZ had just gone through a major downsizing-and-restructuring program. It had many newly created jobs and multiple candidates for each. In the new scheme of things, no one was earmarked for a particular job, and the candidates tended to be part of a group of star performers that the company was trying to match with appropriate jobs. Several executives jointly tried to maximize the fit of a group of people to a set of newly created jobs.

The Reality: There Is No Such Thing as a Typical Promotion

The categorization we have just described may not be highly generalizable. It reflects the small samples gathered from the three companies we studied at this particular point in time. Although we wouldn't expect to consistently find these five types, we would expect that any similar study would find considerable variation in promotions. Promotion is not a unilateral phenomenon: It can differ according to developmental emphasis, nature of the change in job, the role of corporate objectives, whether someone has been earmarked for the job, current characteristics of the industry, and the role of strategic reorganizations in developing the vacancy. At the levels of management studied here, there was no such thing as a typical promotion.

Statement 6:
Most Organizations Use Similar Criteria for Promotion

Based on the assumption that individual attributes predict work perfor-mance, many models of managerial competencies have been developed. Most research and popular articles dealing with career advancement do not take differences across companies into account, thereby giving the impression that there is a standard set of qualifications for people who want to get ahead in corporate America. Our study, because it was conducted in three large corpo-rations, made it possible to see if promotion dynamics were explained differ-ently across companies. The three companies differed in terms of industry, technology, formal succession-planning systems, and organizational culture. Our data suggest that these differences influenced the explanations for promotions.

We found that although the three companies wanted many of the same virtues in their managers (for instance, they wanted change agents with good interpersonal skills and exceptional track records), the companies differed in what they valued. To get at these differences we compared the companies with respect to both the information about their succession-planning system and the reasons for the promotions. Table 1 shows how the frequencies of reasons mentioned differ across the three companies. The differences dis-cussed are statistically significant.

XYZ produces a highly complex technological product that must be extremely reliable—failure of a single unit could result in the loss of lives. The technology is complicated and intensive. Virtually all of its managers are engineers. It is not unusual for a single project to last over twenty years. The company has a formal succession system that was three years old at the time of our study. The succession policy requires decision-makers to review people in line for upper-level positions and to discuss possible positions and developmental needs. Most middle managers are not reviewed. Human resource representatives participate in the promotion process primarily by handling the administrative end; they do not get involved in the actual deci-sions. Bosses tend to promote people they have known for a long time.

With respect to the explanations for promotion, this company puts much more emphasis on technical skills than the other two companies. Virtually everyone promoted was described as a technical whiz. The ability to lead a group was also frequently mentioned as a key factor. The bosses tended to look for people who had already proven they were capable for the job in terms of technical and leadership skills.

MNO differs sharply from XYZ in that it produces industrial and consumer products. It has technologies ranging from routine applications of tried-and-true technologies to cutting-edge systems. Like XYZ, it has a succession-planning system, in place for about ten years at the time of our study. Also like XYZ, it reviews all upper-level managers and positions; in addition, however, it also reviews all supervisory and middle-level managers. Human resource representatives are active in the people-review discussions. It also has a rudimentary career-planning system in parts of the corporation; this allows motivated managers to receive guidance in this area. Senior executives are influential in making promotion decisions at lower levels. The company actively encourages middle managers to place candidates with long-term potential.

The criteria taken into account at MNO reflect some of its differences from XYZ. Although both value track record and want managers who have achieved results in the past, they differ in the emphasis on other factors. MNO emphasizes technical skills less. In most divisions the technology is such that someone can discuss business without being the leading technological specialist. (In XYZ, being able to actively perfect the technology is part of the business advantage.) MNO tends to have a longer time frame on its promotion decisions. It emphasizes, in its words, "intelligence," or raw street smarts, much more than XYZ. Part of the explanation for this is MNO's more substantial developmental orientation; part of it is the role senior management plays in the decisions; and part of it is the fact that the technology allows people with demonstrated intellectual ability, and not just technical knowledge, to excel. In addition, MNO values style, or presentation skills, more than XYZ.

ABC also specializes in industrial and consumer products. Its technology ranges from the traditional tried-and-true to some highly advanced methodologies. Although it is largely staffed by engineers, it does have non-engineers in some managerial positions. The succession-planning system in one form or another has been in place for years. Every year the potential of first-level supervisors and above is discussed in a series of human-resource review sessions. In addition to succession planning, ABC also puts a strong emphasis on career counseling; management candidates are given considerable feedback about their performance and chances for progress, and talented people are nurtured. Neither XYZ nor MNO emphasizes career planning as strongly.

We found that promotions at ABC tend to blend the individual's goals with the organization's needs. Bosses act as both career coaches to individuals and as contributors to the succession-planning process. They help subordinates plan for future possibilities and also provide input on those individuals to their superiors at succession-planning time. Human resource representatives play a key role in both the succession-planning and career-counseling process. They provide guidance to managers interested in moving upwards and often act as talent scouts for bosses, helping them find and evaluate promotion candidates.

The criteria ABC values most highly are a mix of those valued at the two other organizations. Technical competence is valued, but not as highly as at XYZ. Intelligence is also valued, but not as highly as at MNO. ABC seems to seek out a balance between technical experts and people with raw potential. It also takes contextual factors into greater account than the other two companies: Specifically, it is more concerned with diversity than XYZ, and it makes promotions based on being at the right place at the right time and on continuity more than MNO does. The promotions at ABC could be characterized as blending the individual and organization's needs more effectively than at either of the other two companies. This is most likely a reflection of its succession-planning and career-counseling programs.

Another difference between ABC and XYZ is the emphasis on character or personal strength. Personal strength is valued much more at XYZ than at ABC. Because assessment of personal strength is much less important at ABC, it tends to take a greater variety of factors into account in promotions.

In summary, the differences among the three organizations reflect how important it is for career information to be specific to a particular company. Although there are many commonalities across the three companies, there are noticeable differences in the qualities valued by each, illustrating the importance of taking organizational context into account when trying to understand promotions.

A More Realistic Perspective

Our study supports the rational perspective with respect to its heavy emphasis on the individual attributes of candidates. We found that individual attributes such as work ethic, preparation, and achieved results, as well as potential and people skills, figured prominently in promotion decisions. Bosses used these qualities to explain why a particular candidate was selected and in doing so suggested they believe these qualities predict future work performance. Thus the practice of the bosses strongly supports an understanding of promotion based on predictable characteristics of individuals.

Other data in this study, however, suggest that this view of promotion is incomplete. One way that it is lacking is in its neglect of the short- and long-term demands of the department and organization that bear on the promotion decision—for instance, the opportunity structure, the messages sent by promotions, and long-range staffing goals. We found that these contextual factors played a key role. Although they are not totally ignored in the rational perspective (job demands clearly are taken into account), these situational factors played a bigger role in the decisions than the rational perspective accounts for. Bosses emphasized these reasons quite strongly. The rational perspective explains why a particular person was promoted; the contextual reasons address specifically why a person was chosen at a particular time and place. These reasons tie promotions to basic issues of organizational strategy.

The rational perspective is also incomplete with respect to the role of politics in promotion. Ferris et al. (1992) and Herriot, Pemberton, and Pinder (1992) have identified a political perspective which sees the promotion process as one of social negotiation in which promotions are based on connections and interpersonal influence strategies. Our study suggests that these social/political concerns do play a key role in promotions. One way that we found politics entered into the promotion process was through identification of candidates. Who was visible when a promotion was in the works was influenced by social relationships; the candidates either directly knew the hiring manager or had someone act as an advocate for them. We found only a few cases when an employee was identified by a formal system. Who got ahead was a combination of effort, ability, and being known. Promotion was thus a mix of what a person knew and who knew the person.

Another way that politics entered into the process was in assessment. In contrast to the objective assessment suggested by the rational view, our study found that bosses relied on an intuitive, subjective evaluation process based on a combination of factors. Typically bosses looked at accomplishments, intelligence, and their own personal comfort with the candidate. Although accomplishments were sometimes objectively assessed, bosses had difficulty parceling out the contributions of a particular individual in a complicated business situation with a long time-span and multiple players. Bosses often felt they could assess intelligence; however, their descriptions of intelligence appear to confuse glibness with actual smarts. Personal comfort as a measure of assessment obviously reflects social and political considerations and notions of "fit." Basically, the bosses who mentioned comfort said they wanted someone they could feel completely comfortable with and trusting of. They were looking for people they felt connected to, who could influence others, and who were credible to upper management.

The promoted people also recognized that comfort was important. Judge and Ferris (1992) have suggested that both candidates and decision-makers engage in a dynamic political process. Candidates can attempt to alter and manage others' images of their competence and qualifications. Decision-makers may believe they are hiring based on perceived fit with the job when in reality their decisions are the result of, at least in part, perceived similarity to self in terms of interests, values, attitudes, personality, appearance, background, or function. Decision-makers may try to increase their own power by seeking out and building coalitions with people who think like they do and who fit their own personal agendas (Judge & Ferris, 1992; Kanter, 1977). Thus, political concerns may color judgment of individual capabilities. This is not to suggest that politics are all bad; some of these concerns may be relevant to chemistry and effective working relationships between people.

Yet another way that the promotion process described here did not conform to the rational perspective is in the way promotion was understood. The rational perspective sees the organization as being in the powerful role of selector and the candidate in the less powerful role of applicant. It assumes a job with fixed properties that an applicant must somehow "fit." The organization "selects" the individual. The data reported here suggest that promotion is a process of mutual accommodation and social negotiation rather than one of simply matching existing people and opportunities. Bosses and candidates work together to shape the job. Candidates help to "select" positions. This fits with Herriot's (1989) argument that selection is a reciprocal process in which the individual and the organization work together to develop appropriate roles. Future models of promotion need to recognize this process of accommodation.

In summary, our study suggests that promotion processes are extremely complex and need to be viewed from multiple perspectives. The examples we have given reveal how varied the reasons for promotion may be and highlight the difficulty of generalizing about the promotion process. Some of the reasons bosses gave about why they promoted someone can be accounted for in terms of the rational perspective. Our data, however, suggest that this view is only partially complete. Other political, social, and contextual factors are also important. Promotions are negotiated realities taking a wealth of factors into account. Both merit and politics play key roles. Promoted managers are both talented and politically capable. Jobs are adapted to fit candidates and variations in the process exist across companies. Selection and development may or may not be intertwined, depending upon the company's goals and values. Future research needs to be done to better understand the complexities of promotion that we have identified. In doing so, researchers and practitioners alike can go beyond simplistic notions of promotion and see it more realistically as a complicated blend of organizational forces.

Implications

As the above discussion has illustrated, the realities of promotion are quite complex, blending competencies, situational factors, and political skills. This view has implications for the practical situation of both individuals and organizations as well as for further study.

For the Individual

Perhaps the most important implication for the individual relates to feelings of discouragement that one may have if promotions are slow in coming. Lawrence (1984) noted that people who feel that they are behind in their career advancement feel negatively towards the organization. Morrison (1991) has found that Navy officers passed over for promotion are likely to consider leaving. Departure may be a desired result if the organization equates poor performance with a lack of promotions. The data discussed here, however, suggest that performance isn't always the driving force behind promotions. Contextual factors influenced many of the cases we studied. Many capable people may be inadvertently discouraged by the promotion process. A manager may construe not being promoted as a reflection of his or her lack of ability rather than as the lack of available opportunities. These managers need to get feedback about whether the decision truly is a reflection of a lack of ability.

An additional implication for the individual is that people should use an understanding of the role of contextual factors to be in the right place at the right time. Some of the managers we interviewed suggested that their promotions resulted from extra responsibilities and challenges that they had taken on in their previous jobs. One manager, for example, volunteered to help his newly promoted boss with certain responsibilities and when the boss created a new job, the helpful manager was the obvious choice. Managers looking to progress can further their careers by reaching out beyond their assigned responsibilities, thereby influencing their exposure to key opportunities.

Being visible is another way an individual can improve the likelihood of promotion. Executives can't promote people they are not aware of. Several of the promoted managers in the study had taken actions to increase their visibility. They networked: They volunteered to be on task forces, attended events where important people were likely to be, took on new responsibilities, and generally looked for "significant moments" in the course of their work life that could be used to get to know others with decision-making authority.

It is important, however, to point out that using networks to achieve visibility for its own sake alone doesn't work. We didn't find people putting themselves forward simply to be seen by higher-ups. Rather we saw managers engaged in critical business activities with the side benefit of making others aware of their talents. Visibility means more than just being seen—it means allowing others to see your talents in meaningful settings.

Another strategy the promoted managers used was getting feedback. At ABC in particular, promoted managers had talked to others to find out about potential career roadblocks and how to overcome them. One woman clearly saw her most recent promotion as an acknowledgment of having responded to earlier feedback. Responding to feedback indicates to others that you are both able to learn from experience and willing to change.

And finally, and perhaps most importantly, the promoted managers got results. They worked hard to improve the function or department they managed. Others looking to get ahead should remember that a high proportion of the promoted managers had significantly improved an existing situation by creating something new such as a product or function, by fixing an existing business problem, or by fine-tuning an already smooth-running operation.

For the Organization

A key implication for organizations is that they need to pay attention to and examine the contextual features of promotion systems. It is important for an organization to examine whether its de facto system is congruent with organizational objectives. Are the "right" contextual reasons emphasized? How are opportunities developed? What messages are sent by promotion? Are the desired corporate-staffing objectives emphasized? Organizations need to look at the consequences of current practices and extrapolate into the future. Upon receiving feedback from the study, XYZ found our explanation of the criteria it used in promotions to be helpful in increasing its emphasis on development. This company tended to emphasize skills needed in the short term and realized that to stay competitive developmental goals needed greater weight.

A related point is that organizations need to look at the type and mix of their promotions. How many have been promotions in place? How are these used? How often is there a mentor involved? How do bosses justify promotions in place? Organizations also need to examine the number of situations where there is no obvious optimal candidate and decide if this is a reflection of poor developmental preparation or a reflection of many good candidates. In addition, organizations should study cross-divisional moves. How often do they occur? Do they reflect desired long-term staffing goals? Do they require intervention from higher levels of the organization to happen? Under what conditions do developmental promotions occur? Once these and similar questions are answered, human resource specialists can provide better support to executives making decisions. Different support is needed for different types of promotions. The point is, knowledge of the types of promotions used in a particular organization can help executives improve the deployment of staff to achieve strategic goals.

Similarly, organizations also need to pay attention to the ways promotions differ for blacks and whites, women and men. Are different reasons taken into account in these promotions? Do these reasons show appropriate exercise of discretion or do they show subtle discrimination? We found that bosses moved cautiously with promotions for white women and black men; we think that this is because they were so intent on seeing them succeed. Although this has the positive side of giving the organization the chance to see white women and black men perform well, it also forms part of a vicious cycle. The managers who are treated cautiously become less eligible for future jobs because they haven't had the opportunity for the really big successes that come from being handed a risky situation. Organizations concerned with creating and maintaining a diverse work force need to understand the subtle differences between promotions of different groups to see if they agree with basic organizational values.

Another diversity-related concern is the role of comfort level between boss and candidate in promotion. Bosses explained that comfort level had to do with trust and credibility; it meant that the candidate had proven he or she had successfully interacted with upper management in the past. These certainly are important considerations. However, to the extent comfort level translates into "the candidate is like me," it can cause quite a problem. If white-male bosses rely too much on comfort level, the chance of non-whites and females to get ahead is reduced. Kanter (1977) argued that organizations show a preference for homogeneity which she calls "homosocial reproduction," the hiring of people "like me." To the extent that *comfort level* is a euphemism for *homosocial reproduction* it becomes an important point to consider in the implementation of diversity initiatives.

Another area for organizational consideration is how decision-makers make judgments. Our study suggests that individual decision-makers have considerable say in the judgment of talent. To improve the process of predicting who will handle a promotion effectively, it would be helpful if decision-makers had training in assessment. Executives should learn basic principles of behavioral observation and should also be alerted to potential traps in making predictions about people. For example, a possible problem in determining talent is that managers can be insensitive to the predictive power of information in making a decision (Ruderman & Ohlott, 1990). We found cases where bosses inferred someone would be a good manager of others on the basis of an individual technical accomplishment. The bosses used individual accomplishment as a rationale for why the manager would manage subordinates well. People who make such inferences need to be aware that skill as an individual contributor doesn't necessarily translate into supervisory competence.

A further way the prediction process could be improved is if human resource representatives act as sounding boards and talent scouts in the decision-making process. As sounding boards they can help decision-makers consider relevant variables. At ABC the human resource representatives engaged in a dialogue with hiring bosses to get them to consider key variables about the job, the department, the organization, and the candidate. This questioning process helped the decision-makers think through who they wanted for a particular position.

As talent scouts, human resource representatives can help to make more people visible to decision-makers. Prior background with the boss or the boss's boss was characteristic of many of the cases (48%; see Table 2). In part, this was important because the superior thus had information from which to make judgments about the candidate; but it was also important because the prior relationship made the candidate visible. In some of the cases the bosses we interviewed acknowledged that a helpful human resource specialist made them aware of the candidate eventually selected; the bosses were thankful they had such input.

Promotion decisions may also have implications for the design of organizations. Executives, and even human resource representatives, are rarely trained in organization design, yet general managers routinely, albeit intuitively, practice organization design and redesign (Lewin & Stephens, 1993). To a certain extent, managers making promotion decisions are affecting the design of their organizations. Organization design encompasses not only formal organizational structure but also culture, decision-making norms, ethics, information processing, strategy, and the structure of the employment relationship (Daft & Lewin, 1990). When managers reorganize a group and choose a new person to head it, create new jobs, change existing jobs, or decide not to fill others, they are in effect changing the design of their organizations. As organizations moving into the twenty-first century face increasingly turbulent environments, demographic changes, pressure to meet economic goals, and quantum technological changes, they will need to turn to organization design as a source of competitive advantage and success (Lewin & Stephens, 1993). The optimal organization design of the future may be radically different than in the past. Thus, executives who make promotions need to think of each decision not as an isolated incident but as a piece of a larger puzzle in which organizational challenges are also involved.

For Future Research

Our study suggests that researchers should revise their approaches to, and measurement of, promotion. First, we think there needs to be a greater recognition of its many purposes, such as placing surplus talent, implementing strategic agendas, and developing talent. Yet studies which use promotion as a predictor or outcome variable don't consider these different goals. Future research should also take the type of promotion into account. For example, research on the motivating impact of promotion may want to treat those promotions resulting from a reorganization differently from those intended to develop high-potentials for higher levels of responsibility.

A related issue is the relationship between the views of participants in promotions and the data in the records. Our study used both as inputs. The records data implied that most promotions were somehow equal—the majority of them moved the candidate one level in the pay scale. Yet the interview data suggest that the managers viewed them differently. Some saw the single-level increment as a much bigger move than others. Some increases were associated with critical changes in the level of accountability and some were not. This substantiates the findings of other researchers who found discrepancies between records data and self-reports of promotion (Beehr & Juntunen, 1990). The difference between these makes it advisable that future research use both records and perceptual data to ensure that researchers and managers are talking about the same phenomena.

Another direction for further research suggested by this study relates to the individual competencies associated with career advancement. In the past, most studies of career advancement focused on the contributions of the individual (for instance, Howard & Bray, 1988). A considerable body of knowledge has been developed about the competencies needed to achieve success in corporate America (see Beatty, Schneier, & McEvoy, 1987, for a review of the literature). Although the results of these studies have important implications for the development of executives, they leave out a piece of the picture, the piece having to do with the situational determinants of promotion. Future research needs to look at how individual characteristics interact with the situational variables identified in our study. For example, can a high level of managerial competence compensate for being placed in a position of low visibility during a reorganization? We believe that using a more complete model of promotion would result in a better understanding of individual attributes; this, in turn, could lead to improved development-and-selection efforts.

A further avenue for research suggested by this study concerns the ability of decision-makers to judge the managerial talent of others. Our study—as well as the studies reported by Morrow, McElroy, Stamper, and Wilson (1990) and Quinn, Tabor, and Gordon (1968)—seems to indicate that decision-makers vary in their abilities for judging managerial talent. It would be helpful to develop a better understanding of how this ability varies. Research could look at what skills good judges use and at how bias creeps in. Results from this could be used both for training executives and for selecting executives.

Another issue that needs further research is effectiveness. One might argue that without knowledge of the effectiveness of the promotion decisions, it is difficult to make the leap from describing what the process is to prescribing what the process ought to be. Evaluating effectiveness is a common research problem. Although we did ask decision-makers how successful they felt the promotions were, most had great difficulty answering this question. Often they gave answers such as, "It's too soon to tell." This difficulty reflects both the complexity and variability of the promotion process and the problem of establishing criteria for success. For example, one decision-maker may feel the decision was a success because the candidate effectively implemented a change. A second decision-maker with long-term goals in mind may feel it is too early to judge the same person, because the extent of the individual's development is as yet unclear. Or an individual may be successful while the organization may be in trouble, or vice versa. Future research is needed to investigate how people are effective and what criteria should be used for evaluation.

Finally, a fruitful area for research would be to study promotions as an indicator of shifts in strategic direction. In our research we found that several of the cases were part of major organizational shifts in direction. Sometimes the structural change was made to emphasize a particular function. In two of the companies, MNO and ABC, there were promotions that were part of an increasing drive to have a more diverse organizational population. The point is, identifying who got promoted and why appears to be a useful way to trace policy changes. Future research may want to use promotions as a way of analyzing implementation of corporate objectives.

Appendix:
Research Method and Data Analysis

Original Inquiry

How do managers make promotion decisions? We combined record-based and qualitative information to investigate this question in sixty-four promotion decisions made at three different Fortune 500 companies.

Identification of Decisions

The participating organizations were selected on the basis of three criteria. First, they had a strong interest in understanding promotion processes and an interest in improving assignment-management practices. Second, we had to be allowed to study actual promotion decisions, an inherently sensitive topic. All three organizations have had a long and close relationship with the Center for Creative Leadership and were open to the idea of sharing delicate data with the researchers as long as confidentiality was assured. Third, we deliberately selected three companies that rely on different basic technologies and which have different formal approaches to career planning.

In each company we worked with senior human-resource professionals to identify typical promotions that had occurred between 1987 and 1989. We selected this time frame because it covered the twenty-four months prior to the interview phase of the study. Our organizational contacts were asked to define "typical promotions" as job changes in which a manager advanced one or more organizational levels and in which the decision process was considered to be characteristic of the company. They were also asked to choose cases from a variety of representative businesses or functions and from different upper-management levels.

Sample

In order to get a broad view of promotions, we looked at recent cases from three different managerial levels. The highest level was general manager or its equivalent (sixteen cases). These sixteen cases represent almost total sampling of promotions to general management at all three companies during the two-year period we studied. The second level consisted of people who reported to general managers (twenty-four cases). They had titles such as "director" or "plant manager." The third level included people two levels below general manager (twenty-four cases). They had titles such as "business manager" or "project manager."

Approximately 36% of the cases were promotions to staff jobs; 62% were promotions to line jobs; and 2% of the jobs could not be classified as clearly one or the other. Of the managers promoted, forty were white men, sixteen were white women, seven were black men, and one was a black woman. The average age of the promoted managers was forty, and the average company tenure was thirteen years.

Data Collection

Semi-structured interviews were conducted with a number of people familiar with each case in order to develop a composite picture of each decision. Most of the interviews were conducted on-site at the companies; some were conducted by telephone. An interview typically lasted about 90 minutes. Each interviewer took notes during the interview; these were later transcribed. Interviewers had a basic list of questions to ask and were instructed to probe further to learn more about interesting comments.

For each promotion decision, members of the promoted manager's "role set" (Merton, 1957) who were likely to have been influential in the promotion decision were interviewed to provide multiple perspectives on the circumstances surrounding the decision. In most cases the researchers interviewed the promoted person, the immediate supervisor of the promoted person, and the approving boss. In forty-six cases (72%), a human resource representative familiar with the case was also interviewed. In the cases where we did not interview a human resource representative, it was because there wasn't one familiar with the case. The interviews with the decision-makers (the hiring boss and the approving boss) covered their relationship with the candidate, reasons for promotion, information sources, misgivings about the promotion, and information about other candidates. The interviews with the people promoted covered career histories, promotion experiences, and relationships with the decision-makers. Human resource representatives were asked what role they played in the process and their perceptions of the boss-promotee dynamics.

In addition to the interviews, we were also given access to performance appraisals and succession-planning documents relevant to the promotions. The present report focuses on the responses of decision-makers and human resource representatives to the following questions.

Primary Questions

We asked decision-makers (the boss and the boss's boss) the following questions about the person promoted and the promotion decision:

(1) Tell me about how you decided to place _____ in this position. When did the vacancy arise? How did the vacancy arise?

(2) What are the major responsibilities facing _____?

(3) For how long have you known _____? When did you first meet? How did you first hear of _____?

(4) If you were restricted to only one reason why you selected _____ for this position, what would it be? What would a second reason be? Other reasons?

(5) What was it that brought _____ to your attention for this position?

(6) Were there other candidates for the position? Why weren't they selected?

(7) How did you get information about the candidates?

(8) Was this promotion a success?

We asked similar questions of the people promoted:

(1) What is your current job? What are its duties and responsibilities?

(2) What people do you think had a part in your promotion decision? How long have you known each of them? What is your relationship to each of them?

(3) If you were allowed to describe only one reason why you think you were selected for this position, what would it be? How do you know that? When do you think people first realized that about you?

(4) What would a second reason be? Any other reasons?

(5) Who else was considered for your job? Why do you think they were not selected?

Human resource managers familiar with the cases were asked:

(1)   What is _____'s background? What are _____'s major
        responsibilities in this job?

(2)   How did the vacancy occur?

(3)   Who was involved in the promotion decision?

(4)   Was anyone else considered for the position? Why weren't they
        selected?

(5)   What was the single most important reason _____ was
        promoted?

(6)   What were other reasons?

Data Analysis

This study was designed not to test specific hypotheses but to develop a better understanding of the promotion process so that new theories could be generated. Following the logic of inductive research (Glaser & Strauss, 1967; Yin, 1989), conceptual categorization and data analysis proceeded simultaneously, allowing for the constant comparison of data and coding categories. Our first task was to build an understanding of promotion processes and to develop coding categories; the second was to quantify and present the data in these categories.

Category- and interpretation-building. While the data was being collected at the first site, we transcribed the interview notes and repeatedly read them to identify key ideas. For each of the fifteen decisions at the first site, we developed a promotion profile, a four- to five-page summary of the key events in the promotion that consolidated the information we obtained from different sources. We then looked across the promotion profiles for similarities and differences and we documented key features of the promotion process. From these, we developed the initial two categorization schemes. One categorization scheme involved the reasons for promotions. The second categorization scheme placed promotions in groups based on similarities and differences across the cases. We also developed a listing of ways candidates became visible to decision-makers.

Next, we went back to the individual cases and coded them into categories, modifying the categories as required. Two coders jointly developed the categories and then independently coded the data. Disagreements were argued to consensus and the coding categories refined. These categories were then shared with our corporate contacts and some of the actual executives interviewed. They provided a reality check for the codings and discussed with us distinctions between the different categories, which led to refinements in the category definitions.

The data collected at the second site was transcribed, summarized, and sorted into the existing categories on the basis of the summaries. New categories were created to account for newly acquired data. Old ones were modified to better reflect promotion dynamics. Two coders jointly coded the data, arguing differences of opinion to consensus. The coding scheme was then shared with our corporate contacts and study participants at the second site, whose comments led to slight revisions. At the third site the process was repeated.

After looking at the data from the third site, we finalized the categories. At this point we also developed a list of dichotomous questions about the circumstances of the promotions. These questions were sometimes redundant with the information in the reasons for promotion, but we specifically wanted to pull these issues out of the data for further analyses.

The final phase of the coding consisted of returning to the data from the first and second sites and reanalyzing them in terms of the final set of categories, concepts, and questions. Each case could have multiple reasons for promotion, but each case was coded into only one category in the typology of promotion types.

After the categories were developed and the codings completed, in order to ensure the accuracy of the coding, an independent reviewer was trained in the coding process and then coded a random sample of the cases. The independent coder was given category definitions, examples of data in each category, and was asked to code sixteen cases. There was 88% interrater agreement in the coding of factors and circumstances. Interrater agreement on the typology was somewhat lower (50%), in part because we had only sixteen cases to code, with each case coded into one of the five categories, and the independent coder tended to favor the developmental category; perhaps our category descriptions were not clear or we did not provide sufficient training to the coder.

Presentation of results. All of our codings were entered into the computer as dichotomous variables, and SAS was used to compute frequencies. Chi-square analyses and phi coefficients were computed where appropriate to examine company differences in the quantitative data. Table 1 shows reasons given for promotions overall and by company. Circumstances surrounding promotions are presented in Table 2. Our typology of promotions appears in Table 3.

In addition, as we read each case, we asked ourselves a number of qualitative questions to help us make judgments about it (for example: "Where did the decision-maker get information about the person?" "Does this case tell us anything about job customization?" "How long has the candidate known the hiring boss?"). Research team members discussed each case and what was learned from it by attending to these questions. Responses to these questions were entered into the qualitative-analysis program askSam® and responses were aggregated. These interpretive comments helped us keep track of our impressions and learnings from every single case and provided us with valuable examples, many of which are given in the text of this report.

Figure 1
FACTORS IN PROMOTION:
DEFINITIONS USED IN THE STUDY

Preparation

Track Record of Success: The person had a track record of succeeding in projects, indicating he or she has been tested and proven.

Change Agent: The candidate has successfully implemented a change in the past thereby improving a situation. The change may be in any arena: technological, administrative, quality, interpersonal, managerial, commercial, or manufacturing. Results-oriented, proactive.

Right Combination of Credentials: The person had the right blend of experiences, training, and competencies for the job.

Broad Knowledge of the Organization: Experience in the organization has been varied and provides a basis for understanding events outside the home division. Understands the culture, what makes the company tick. Knows where bodies are buried, who knows what.

Experience Adds Utility to Group: The candidate brought an experience that added to the collective expertise of the group.

Technical Skills: Outstanding expertise in a functional area.

Readiness: Person has put in the appropriate amount of time. Has paid his/her dues. Has been there long enough. Recognition for work already done.

Attitudes

Work Ethic: The candidate demonstrated commitment to the company, department, or product with lots of initiative and a can-do attitude. Showed an eagerness to get things done. Dedicated.

Good Citizen of the Organization: The candidate has made contributions outside the scope of his or her job such as recruiting minorities, acting as a mentor, or championing a company-wide initiative.

People Skills

Interpersonal Skills: The person's strong interpersonal and communication skills were noted in a general way.

Team Player: Someone who would be accepted by other members of the staff and would add value to the team.

Team Builder/Leadership: The person is able to demonstrate the ability to get people committed and to work together as part of a team without kicking them in the process. Able to coach and develop people. Can mobilize and marshal people to achieve a goal.

Influence Skills: The candidate has credibility with other units, customers, partners, or industry representatives and can effectively interface with them.

Comfort Level With Superiors/Known Quantity: The person was a known entity to the boss or his or her superiors and had proved that he or she could success-fully interface with them. The boss was comfortable with and had trust in the promotion candidate. Credible to upper levels of management.

Emotional Competence: Demonstration of genuine sensitivity and caring for others.

Personal Attributes

Intelligence: Exercise of good judgment, articulate, bright, able to extract the essence of complex situations. Quick on one's feet.

Analytical Abilities: Rational and practical when making decisions.

Potential for Growth: The capacity for growth has been demonstrated and the person is considered to be someone who has the possibility for further advance-ment in the system. Able to pick up new knowledge.

Creative: Innovative problem-solving abilities. A novel thinker who sees new directions and possibilities.

Personal Strength/Character: Demonstration of a willingness to take risks, maturity, acceptance of responsibility, able to handle tough business decisions. Able to challenge superiors when necessary. Self-confidence in uncharted waters, speaks own mind.

Style: Presence, stature, shows sizzle in presentations. Projects an image of a leader, smooth. Good socializer.

Business Smarts: Has a strong sense of the business and how to identify and solve business problems. A sixth sense for making deals. Able to read customer requirements and turn them into plans.

Accountable and Responsible: Follows through relentlessly; detailed understanding of responsibilities. High integrity.

Able to Work the System: Can bring resources together. Can make large organizations respond.

Strategic Thinker: Able to think broadly beyond one's own area to the bigger picture, engages in long-range planning.

Context

Right Place/Right Time: The person happened to have the necessary mix of skills and qualifications at just the time when the job became available.

Groomed for Job: Someone higher in the hierarchy had supported the person during his or her career and had seen that the person had the necessary preparation for this job or one like it. In some cases someone higher than the boss pushed for him or her to be offered the job.

Developmental: The job was seen as a growth opportunity which would develop specific skills or prepare the person for a specific job. In some cases the job was seen as developmental because the boss was good at developing people. In some cases the job was a test or proving ground.

Available: The person had been freed up from previous job responsibilities usually because of some type of reorganization.

Indispensable to Function: The person was essential to the business or project because they had substantial background and history that could not be duplicated.

Pushed for Job: Candidate played a major role in convincing the boss/company he or she is deserving of a promotion.

Equity: The person was promoted in order to be fair to him or her. The person may have been led to believe he or she would be promoted into that job or may have complained to his or her boss that previous incumbents had been at a higher

level. In some cases the promotion was to recognize an increased level of responsibilities or the awkwardness of not having given the person another job.

Retention: A key factor in the promotion was to keep the person in the company
or division and to see that his or her talents were put to good use. In some cases,
they were proven top performers; in others they were simply people with an
exceptional talent.

Diversity: Promoting this person would add to the number of high-level white
women or people of color in leadership roles, supporting the organization's
policies.

Vacancy Demanded Attention: The job had been vacant so long or was vacant at
such a crucial time that the pressures to fill it were overwhelming.

Continuity in Location, Function, or Business: The candidate was an insider who
knows the culture, technology, and values of the organization. Insider status.

Figure 2
TYPES OF PROMOTIONS

Developmental

The promotion is designed to prepare the person for key positions in the future. The job may provide someone headed for derailment with a second chance. Or it may be part of a natural progression of opportunities in that the candidate has been groomed for this job, or one like it, and is being prepared for higher advancement possibilities. Less frequently, the person may be unprepared for the job in a significant way but is given the opportunity in order to gain a perspective or skill necessary for further advancement.

Promotions in Place

In this type of promotion, only one person is considered for the job. In some situations, the candidate is promised a promotion if he or she takes on the responsibilities of the job at a certain level and performs well. In these cases, promotion occurs to fulfill the promise, recognize quality performance, and sometimes correct inequity in pay compared to relevant others. In other cases, the scope of the job has increased and for reasons of continuity it is important to keep the person in place and to recognize the added responsibilities with a promotion.

No Obvious Optimal Candidate

In an absence of an obviously qualified candidate, decision-makers must act to find a suitable candidate. Sometimes, an extensive search is made in order to find a single stellar candidate. In other cases, a search may be conducted through which several good candidates emerge and are compared to each other, with the best available candidate getting the job. Sometimes, the formal system plays a critical role in discovering the candidate. In other cases, there are no optimal candidates and every contender is a risk; the best of these non-optimal candidates is selected.

Organizational Objectives

These promotions involve long-term corporate objectives, such as long-range staffing, diversity, or strategic goals. Human resource or higher-level executives are often involved in the decisions. These types of promotions sometimes occur when people who become available need to be placed or when talented performers suggest they are thinking about leaving the organization.

Reorganizations

Reorganizations are a major source of promotions. Sometimes, because of centralization or decentralization of a function, the job has been moved organizationally but the basic content of the job remains the same. Other times, a group of candidates are considered to fill a set of new or revised positions. In some cases reorganizations simply add new responsibilities to the job's original ones.

Table 1
FACTORS IN PROMOTIONS

Factor	Percentage of the 64 Cases Overall	Percentage of the ABC Cases	Percentage of the MNO Cases	Percentage of the XYZ Cases
Preparation				
Track record of success	61	63	64	53
Change agent	36	43	28	27
Right combination of credentials	30	31	14	40
Broad knowledge of the organization	20	23	14	20
Experience adds utility to group	30	29	29	33
Technical skills	50	49	14	87
Readiness	20	34	0	7
Attitudes				
Work ethic	38	46	14	40
Good citizen of the organization	3	3	7	0
People Skills				
Interpersonal skills	45	43	57	40
Team player	14	17	7	13
Team builder/Leadership	47	37	43	73
Influence skills	39	40	36	40
Comfort level with superiors/ Known quantity	44	49	36	40
Emotional competence	5	6	0	7
Personal Attributes				
Intelligence	45	37	93	20
Analytical abilities	8	11	7	0
Potential for growth	59	54	79	53
Creative	11	17	0	7
Personal strength/Character	29	17	43	47
Style	20	11	50	13
Business smarts	17	20	21	7
Accountable and responsible	23	14	21	47
Able to work the system	9	11	0	13
Strategic thinker	19	11	43	13

Table 1 (continued)
FACTORS IN PROMOTIONS

Factor	Percentage of the 64 Cases Overall	Percentage of the ABC Cases	Percentage of the MNO Cases	Percentage of the XYZ Cases
Context				
Right place/Right time	22	29	0	27
Groomed for job	9	17	0	0
Developmental	47	43	79	27
Available	19	23	29	0
Indispensable to function	2	0	0	100
Pushed for job	11	20	0	0
Equity	6	11	0	0
Retention	14	23	7	0
Diversity	30	43	29	0
Vacancy demanded attention	2	0	0	7
Continuity in location, function, or business	20	26	7	20

Note: Each case was coded into multiple categories.

Table 2
CIRCUMSTANCES OF PROMOTIONS

Circumstance	Percentage of Cases
Was there only one *true* candidate?	43
Was the job an expansion of the candidate's previous job?	20
Was person selected the first choice?	89
Did one or more of the decision-makers have *serious* misgivings about the promotion?	22
Did the formal system help to locate this person?	20
Was the promotion part of a reorganization?	48
Was the candidate part of a slate of candidates?	8
Was the candidate available?	20
Were diversity goals a factor?	31
Did candidate previously work for hiring boss?	57
Did candidate previously work for approving boss?	48
Was candidate already working in the department prior to the promotion?	69
Was the prior incumbent promoted?	34
Did someone higher than the immediate boss play a *pivotal* role in the promotion (i.e., did someone significantly influence the boss's decision)?	31
Was the promotion a fulfillment of a promise?	9
Was retention of the candidate an explicit goal of the promotion?	19
Was the job customized for the candidate?	20
Was the job newly created?	31
Was the person promoted groomed for the job?	34

Table 2 (continued)
CIRCUMSTANCES OF PROMOTIONS

Circumstance	Percentage of Cases
Was the promotion a transfer across functional lines?	12
Was the promotion a transfer across business lines?	35
Did the person have either a primary mentor (someone providing sponsorship, coaching, protection, exposure, challenging work, friendship, role modeling, counseling and acceptance and confirmation) or a secondary mentor (someone providing career functions such as occasional advice, exposure, some coaching, etc.)?	81
Was human resources involved in the decision?	52
Was continuity in the department or function an issue?	22
Was the promotion part of a chain of moves?	29

Table 3
TYPOLOGY OF PROMOTIONS

Type	Percentage of the 64 Cases Overall	Percentage of the ABC Cases	Percentage of the MNO Cases	Percentage of the XYZ Cases
Developmental	31	29	43	27
Promotions in Place	14	20	7	7
No Obvious Optimal Candidate	22	14	14	47
Organizational Objectives	25	31	36	0
Reorganizations	8	6	0	20

References

Beatty, R. W., Schneier, C. E., & McEvoy, G. M. (1987). Executive development and management succession. In K. M. Rowland & G. R. Ferris (Eds.), *Research in personnel and human resources management, 5* (pp. 289-322). Greenwich, CT: JAI Press.

Beehr, T. A., & Juntunen, D. L. (1990). Promotions and employees' perceived mobility channels: The effects of employee sex, employee group, and initial placement. *Human Relations, 43*(5), 455-472.

Bentz, V. J. (1990). Contextual issues in predicting high level leadership performance. In K. E. Clark & M. B. Clark (Eds.), *Measures of leadership* (pp. 131-143). West Orange, NJ: Leadership Library of America.

Beyer, J. M., Stevens, J. M., & Trice, H. M. (1980). Predicting how federal managers perceive criteria used for their promotion. *Public Administration Review, 40*(1), 55-66.

Bray, D. W., & Howard, A. (1983). The AT&T longitudinal studies of managers. In K. W. Shaie (Ed.), *Longitudinal studies of adult psychological development* (pp. 266-312). New York: The Guilford Press.

Butterfield, D. A., & Powell, G. N. (1991). *Is the glass ceiling cracking? An empirical study of actual promotions to top management.* Paper presented at the meeting of the Academy of Management, Miami, FL.

Cannings, K. (1988). Managerial promotion: The effects of socialization, specialization and gender. *Industrial and Labor Relations Review, 42*(1), 77-88.

Cannings, K., & Montmarquette, C. (1991). Managerial momentum: A simultaneous model of the career progress of male and female managers. *Industrial and Labor Relations Review, 44*(2), 212-228.

Cook, M. (1988). *Personnel selection and productivity.* New York: John Wiley & Sons.

Daft, R. L., & Lewin, A. Y. (1990). Can organization studies begin to break out of the normal science straitjacket? An editorial essay. *Organization Science, 1,* 1-9.

Derr, C. B., Jones, C., & Toomey, E. L. (1988). Managing high-potential employees: Current practices in thirty-three U.S. corporations. *Human Resource Management, 27*(3), 273-290.

Dobson, J. R. (1988). Seniority promotion systems—a review. *Personnel Review (UK), 17*(5), 19-28.

Eberts, R. W., & Stone, J. A. (1985). Male-female differences in promotions: EEO in public education. *Journal of Human Resources, 20*(4), 504-521.

Ferris, G. R., Buckley, M. R., & Allen, G. M. (1992). Promotion systems in organizations. *Human Resource Planning, 15*(3), 47-68.

Ferris, G. R., & King, T. R. (1991). Politics in human resources decisions: A walk on the dark side. *Organizational Dynamics*, 59-71.

Forbes, J. B. (1987). Early intraorganizational mobility: Patterns and influences. *Academy of Management Journal, 30*(1), 110-125.

Forbes, J. B., & Piercy, J. E. (1991). *Corporate mobility and paths to the top.* Westport, CT: Quorum Books.

Glaser, B., & Strauss, A. (1967). *The discovery of grounded theory.* Chicago: Aldine.

Gold, U., & Pringle, J. (1988). Gender-specific factors in management promotion. *Journal of Managerial Psychology* (UK), *3*(4), 17-22.

Herriot, P. (1989). Selection as social process. In M. Smith & I. T. Robertson (Eds.). *Advances in selection assessment* (pp. 171-187). New York: John Wiley & Sons, Ltd.

Herriot, P., Pemberton, C., & Pinder, R. (1992). Misperceptions by managers and their bosses of each other's preferences regarding the managers' careers: A case of the blind leading the blind? Manuscript under review.

Hough, L. M. (1984). Development and evaluation of the "Accomplishment Record" method of selecting and promoting professionals. *Journal of Applied Psychology, 69*, 135-146.

Howard, A. (1986). College experiences and managerial performance. *Journal of Applied Psychology, 71*, 530-552.

Howard, A., & Bray, D. W. (1988). *Managerial lives in transition: Advancing age and changing times.* New York: Guilford.

Judge, T. A., & Ferris, G. R. (1992). The elusive criterion of fit in human resources staffing decisions. *Human Resource Planning, 15*(4), 47-68.

Kanter, R. M. (1977). *Men and women of the corporation.* New York: Basic Books.

Kennedy, M. M. (1991, July/August). Who gets promoted? *Across the Board*, pp. 54-55.

Lawrence, B. S. (1984). Age grading: The implicit organizational timetable. *Journal of Occupational Behavior, 5*(1), 23-35.

Lee, R. (1985a). The theory and practice of promotion processes: Part one. *Leadership and Organization Development Journal* (UK), *6*, 3-6.

Lee, R. (1985b). The theory and practice of promotion processes: Part two. *Leadership and Organization Development Journal* (UK), *6*(4), 17-21.

Lewin, A. Y., & Stephens, C. U. (1993). Epilogue: Designing post-industrial organizations: Combining theory and practice. In G. P. Huber & W. H. Glick (Eds.), *Organizational change and redesign: Ideas and insights for improving performance* (pp. 393-409). New York: Oxford University Press.

London, M., & Stumpf, S. A. (1983). Effects of candidate characteristics on management promotion decisions: An experimental study. *Personnel Psychology, 36*(2), 241-259.

Markham, W. T., Harlan, S. L., & Hackett, E. J. (1987). Promotion opportunity in organizations: Causes and consequences. In K. M. Rowland & G. R. Ferris (Eds.), *Research in personnel and human resources management, 5.* Greenwich, CT: JAI Press.

McCall, M. W., Lombardo, M. M., & Morrison, A. M. (1988). *The lessons of experience: How successful executives develop on the job.* Lexington, MA: Lexington Books.

Merton, R. (1957). *Social theory and social structure.* New York: The Free Press.

Morrison, R. F. (1991). *The contribution of promotability and perception of promotion opportunity to turnover.* Paper presented at the Academy of Management meeting, Miami, FL.

Morrow, P. C., McElroy, J. C., Stamper, B. G., & Wilson, M. A. (1990). The effects of physical attractiveness and other demographic characteristics on promotion decisions. *Journal of Management, 16*(4), 723-736.

Quinn, R. P., Tabor, J. M., & Gordon, L. K. (1968). *The decision to discriminate: A study of executive selection.* Ann Arbor, MI: Institute for Social Research, University of Michigan.

Robertson, I. T., & Iles, P. A. (1988). Approaches to managerial selection. In C. L. Cooper & I. Robertson (Eds.), *International Review of Industrial and Organizational Psychology,* 159-211.

Rosenbaum, J. E. (1979). Tournament mobility: Career patterns in a corporation. *Administrative Science Quarterly, 24,* 220-241.

Rosenbaum, J. E. (1984). *Career mobility in a corporate hierarchy.* New York: Academic Press.

Rosenbaum, J. E. (1989a). Organizational career mobility: Promotion chances in corporations during periods of growth and contraction. *American Journal of Sociology, 85*(1), 21-47.

Rosenbaum, J. E. (1989b). Organization career systems and employee misperceptions. In M. B. Arthur, D. T. Hall, & B. S. Lawrence (Eds.), *Handbook of career theory.* New York: Cambridge University Press.

Ruderman, M. N., & Ohlott, P. J. (1990). *Traps and pitfalls in the judgment of executive potential.* (Report No. 141). Greensboro, NC: Center for Creative Leadership.

Schneider, B., & Schmitt, N. (1986). *Staffing organizations* (2nd ed.). Glenview, IL: Scott, Foresman.

Stumpf, S. A., & London, M. (1981a). Capturing rater policies in evaluation candidates for promotion. *Academy of Management Journal, 24*(4), 752-766.

Stumpf, S. A., & London, M. (1981b). Management promotions: Individual and organizational factors influencing the decision process. *Academy of Management Review, 6*(4), 539-549.

Taylor, R. N. (1975). Preferences of industrial managers for information sources in making promotion decisions. *Journal of Applied Psychology, 60,* 269-272.

Veiga, J. F. (January-February, 1973). The mobile manager at mid-career. *Harvard Business Review,* 115-119.

Yin, R. (1984). *Case study research.* Beverly Hills, CA: Sage Publications.

OTHER PUBLICATIONS

SELECTED REPORTS:

Off the Track: Why and How Successful Executives Get Derailed
Morgan W. McCall, Jr., & Michael M. Lombardo (1983, Stock #121R) $10.00
High Hurdles: The Challenge of Executive Self-Development
Robert E. Kaplan, Wilfred H. Drath, & Joan R. Kofodimos (1985, Stock #125R) $15.00
Key Events in Executives' Lives
Esther H. Lindsey, Virginia Homes, & Morgan W. McCall, Jr. (1987, Stock #132R) $65.00
**Eighty-eight Assignments for Development in Place: Enhancing the Developmental
Challenge of Existing Jobs**
Michael M. Lombardo & Robert W. Eichinger (1989, Stock #136R) $12.00
Why Executives Lose Their Balance
Joan R. Kofodimos (1989, Stock #137R) $15.00
Preventing Derailment: What To Do Before It's Too Late
Michael M. Lombardo & Robert W. Eichinger (1989, Stock #138R) $20.00
Traps and Pitfalls in the Judgment of Executive Potential
Marian N. Ruderman & Patricia J. Ohlott (1990, Stock #141R) $15.00
**Redefining What's Essential to Business Performance: Pathways to Productivity,
Quality, and Service**
Leonard R. Sayles (1990, Stock #142R) $20.00
**Character Shifts: The Challenge of Improving Executive Performance Through
Personal Growth**
Robert E. Kaplan (1990, Stock #143R) $25.00
Twenty-two Ways to Develop Leadership in Staff Managers
Robert W. Eichinger & Michael M. Lombardo (1990, Stock #144R) $12.00
**Gender Differences in the Development of Managers: How Women Managers
Learn From Experience**
Ellen Van Velsor & Martha W. Hughes (1990, Stock #145R) $30.00
**Effective School Principals: Competencies for Meeting the Demands of
Educational Reform**
Cynthia D. McCauley (1990, Stock #146R) $15.00
The Expansive Executive (Second Edition)
Robert E. Kaplan (1991, Stock #147R) $20.00
Understanding Executive Performance: A Life-Story Perspective
Charles J. Palus, William Nasby, & Randolph D. Easton (1991, Stock #148R) $15.00
Feedback to Managers, Volume I: A Guide to Evaluating Multi-rater Feedback Instruments
Ellen Van Velsor & Jean Brittain Leslie (1991, Stock #149R) $15.00
**Feedback to Managers, Volume II: A Review and Comparison of Sixteen Multi-rater
Feedback Instruments**
Ellen Van Velsor & Jean Brittain Leslie (1991, Stock #150R) $75.00
Feedback to Managers, Volumes I and II
Ellen Van Velsor & Jean Brittain Leslie (1991, Stock #151R) $80.00
Upward-communication Programs in American Industry
Allen I. Kraut & Frank H. Freeman (1992, Stock #152R) $25.00
Training for Action: A New Approach to Executive Development
Robert M. Burnside & Victoria A. Guthrie (1992, Stock #153R) $12.00
Readers' Choice: A Decade of *Issues & Observations*
Wilfred H. Drath, Editor (1990, Stock #314R) $20.00
Coping With an Intolerable Boss
Michael M. Lombardo & Morgan W. McCall, Jr. (1984, Stock #305R) $10.00

Learning How to Learn From Experience: Impact of Stress and Coping
Kerry A. Bunker & Amy D. Webb (1992, Stock #154R) $25.00
The Creative Opportunists: Conversations With the CEOs of Small Businesses
James S. Bruce (1992, Stock #316R) $12.00
Why Managers Have Trouble Empowering: A Theoretical Perspective Based on
Concepts of Adult Development
Wilfred H. Drath (1993, Stock #155R) $12.00

SELECTED BOOKS:

If You Don't Know Where You're Going You'll Probably End Up Somewhere Else
David P. Campbell (1974, Stock #203R) $8.95
Take the Road to Creativity and Get Off Your Dead End
David P. Campbell (1977, Stock #204R) $8.95
If I'm In Charge Here, Why Is Everybody Laughing?
David P. Campbell (1980, Stock #205R) $8.95
**Breaking the Glass Ceiling: Can Women Reach the Top of America's Largest
Corporations? (Updated Edition)**
Ann M. Morrison, Randall P. White, & Ellen Van Velsor (1992, Stock #236R) $19.95
The Lessons of Experience: How Successful Executives Develop on the Job
Morgan W. McCall, Jr., Michael M. Lombardo, & Ann M. Morrison (1988, Stock #211R) $19.95
Measures of Leadership
Kenneth E. Clark & Miriam B. Clark (Eds.) (1990, Stock #215R) $59.50
Beyond Ambition: How Driven Managers Can Lead Better and Live Better
Robert E. Kaplan, Wilfred H. Drath, & Joan R. Kofodimos (1991, Stock #227R) $27.95
Inklings: Collected Columns on Leadership and Creativity
David P. Campbell (1992, Stock #233R) $15.00
Readings in Innovation
Stanley S. Gryskiewicz & David A. Hills (Eds.) (1992, Stock #240R) $20.00
The New Leaders: Guidelines on Leadership Diversity in America
Ann M. Morrison (1992, Stock #238R) $25.95
Impact of Leadership
Kenneth E. Clark, Miriam B. Clark, & David P. Campbell (Eds.) (1992, Stock #235R) $59.50
Developing Diversity in Organizations: A Digest of Selected Literature
Ann M. Morrison & Kristen M. Crabtree (1992, Stock #317R) $20.00
**Healing the Wounds: Overcoming the Trauma of Layoffs and Revitalizing
Downsized Organizations**
David M. Noer (1993, Stock #245R) $22.95
Executive Selection: A Look at What We Know and What We Need to Know
David L. DeVries (1993, Stock #321R) $15.00
**Discovering Creativity: Proceedings of the 1992 International Creativity and Innovation
Networking Conference**
Stanley S. Gryskiewicz (Ed.) (1993, Stock #319R) $25.00
Making Diversity Happen: Controversies and Solutions
Ann M. Morrison, Marian N. Ruderman, & Martha Hughes-James (1993, Stock #320R) $20.00
The Realities of Management Promotion
Marian N. Ruderman & Patricia J. Ohlott (1994, Stock #157R) $15.00

Discounts are available. Please write for a comprehensive Resource Guide (reports, books, videotapes, and audiotapes). Address your request to: Publication, Center for Creative Leadership, P.O. Box 26300, Greensboro, NC 27438-6300, 910-288-7210, ext. 2805. All prices subject to change.

ORDER FORM

Name _____ Title _____

Organization _____

Mailing Address _____

City/State/Zip _____

Telephone _____

Quantity	Stock No.	Title	Unit Cost	Amount

Subtotal	
Shipping and Handling (Add 5% of subtotal–must be at least $3.00)	
All NC Residents add 6% sales tax	
TOTAL	

METHOD OF PAYMENT

❑ Check or money order enclosed (payable to Center for Creative Leadership).

❑ Purchase Order No. _____ (Must be accompanied by this form.)

❑ Charge my order, plus shipping, to my credit card: ❑ VISA ❑ MasterCard
  ❑ American Express ❑ Discover

ACCOUNT NUMBER: _____ EXPIRATION DATE: MO. ____ YR. ____

NAME OF ISSUING BANK: _____

SIGNATURE _____

❑ Please put me on your mailing list.
❑ Please send me the Center's quarterly publication, *Issues & Observations*.

Publication • Center for Creative Leadership • P.O. Box 26300
Greensboro, NC 27438-6300
910-545-2805 • FAX 910-288-3999

fold here

PLACE
STAMP
HERE

CENTER FOR CREATIVE LEADERSHIP
PUBLICATION
P. O. Box 26300
Greensboro, NC 27438-6300